Sports and Activities

Let's Downhill Ski!

by Carol K. Lindeen

Consulting Editor: Gail Saunders-Smith, PhD

Consultant: Kymm Ballard, MA
Physical Education, Athletics, and Sports Medicine Consultant
North Carolina Department of Public Instruction

Capstone
press

Mankato, Minnesota

Pebble Plus is published by Capstone Press,
151 Good Counsel Drive, P.O. Box 669, Mankato, Minnesota 56002.
www.capstonepress.com

1 2 3 4 5 6 11 10 09 08 07 06

Library of Congress Cataloging-in-Publication Data
Lindeen, Carol K., 1976–
Let's downhill ski! / by Carol K. Lindeen.
    p. cm.—(Pebble plus. Sports and activities)
    Summary: "Simple text and photographs present the skills, equipment, and safety concerns of downhill
skiing"—Provided by publisher.
    Includes bibliographical references and index.
    ISBN-13: 978-0-7368-6359-9 (hardcover)
    ISBN-10: 0-7368-6359-1 (hardcover)
    1. Downhill skiing—Juvenile literature. I. Title. II. Series.
GV864.315.L56 2007
796.93'5—dc22   2006000502

Editorial Credits
Amber Bannerman, editor; Juliette Peters, set designer; Bobbi J. Wyss, book designer; Kelly Garvin, photo
    researcher/photo editor

Photo Credits
Capstone Press/TJ Thoraldson, cover, 1, 9, 11, 18–19
Corbis/Ariel Skelley, 16–17; David Stoecklein, 13; Free Agents Limited, 6–7; Randy Faris, 14–15; Tony Demin, 5
Getty Images Inc./Paul Viant, 21

Capstone Press thanks the staff at Mount Kato in Mankato, Minnesota, for their assistance with this book.

Note to Parents and Teachers

The Sports and Activities set supports national physical education standards related
to recognizing movement forms and exhibiting a physically active lifestyle. This
book describes and illustrates downhill skiing. The images support early readers in
understanding the text. The repetition of words and phrases helps early readers learn
new words. This book also introduces early readers to subject-specific vocabulary words,
which are defined in the Glossary section. Early readers may need assistance to read
some words and to use the Table of Contents, Glossary, Read More, Internet Sites, and
Index sections of the book.

Table of Contents

Downhill Skiing

Swoosh, swoosh, swoosh!

It's fun to ski

down a snowy hill.

Ski resorts are
good places to ski.
A ski lift takes skiers
up the hill.

Equipment

Skis come in
different sizes.
The taller you are,
the longer your skis
should be.

Skiers wear ski boots.

A binding holds the boot

to the ski.

binding

Some skiers use poles
to help them turn.
Skiers also use poles
to push themselves
in flat places.

Safety

Warm clothes

keep skiers from getting cold.

Skiers wear goggles

to protect their eyes

from the sun and snow.

Skiers learn how to

turn, slow down,

stop, and fall.

They practice on small slopes.

Skiers obey the posted rules.
They stay off closed trails.
They watch out for
other skiers.

Having Fun

Put on some skis.

Hit the slopes.

Let's downhill ski!

Glossary

binding—the part of the ski that holds the boot to the ski; bindings release the boots when skiers fall.

goggles—tinted glasses that fit tightly around the eyes; goggles protect skiers' eyes from the sun's rays and falling snow.

obey—to do what someone tells you to do

resort—a place to relax and have fun; people go to ski resorts to ski.

ski lift—a machine that brings skiers to the top of a hill for skiing

slope—a hill; people ski on slopes.

Read More

Eckart, Edana. *I Can Ski*. Sports. New York: Children's Press, 2003.

Jones, Melanie Davis. *I Can Ski!* A Rookie Reader. New York: Children's Press, 2003.

Klingel, Cynthia Fitterer. *Downhill Skiing*. Wonder Books. Chanhassen, Minn.: Child's World, 2003.

Internet Sites

FactHound offers a safe, fun way to find Internet sites related to this book. All of the sites on FactHound have been researched by our staff.

Here's how:

1. Visit *www.facthound.com*

2. Choose your grade level.

3. Type in this book ID **0736863591** for age-appropriate sites. You may also browse subjects by clicking on letters, or by clicking on pictures and words.

4. Click on the **Fetch It** button.

FactHound will fetch the best sites for you!

Index

Word Count: 131
Grade: 1
Early-Intervention Level: 14